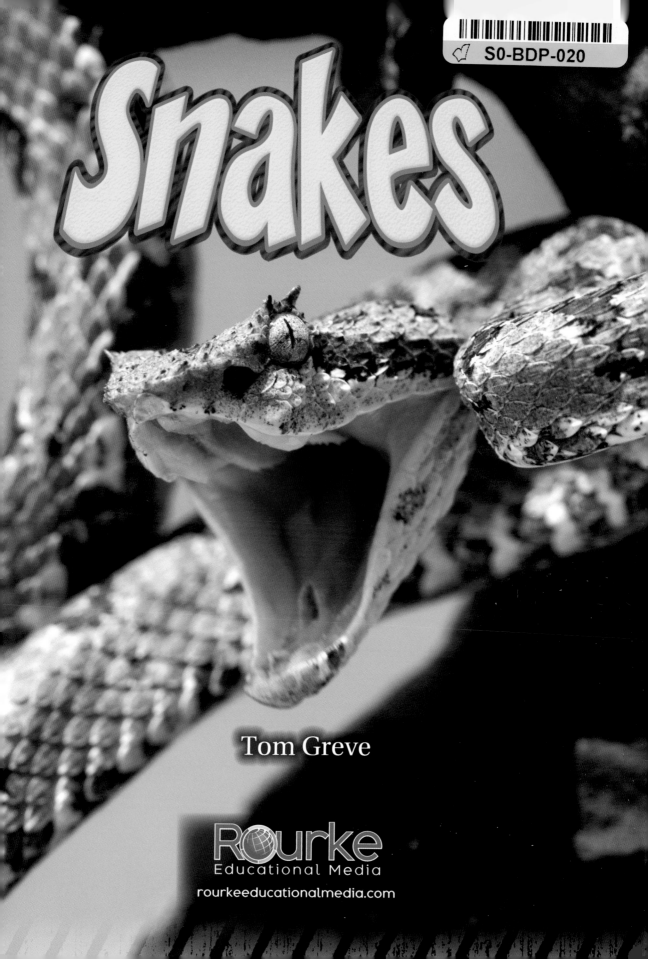

Snakes

Tom Greve

Rourke
Educational Media

rourkeeducationalmedia.com

www.rourkeeducationalmedia.com

PHOTO CREDITS: Cover: © Freedomman; Title Page, 3: © Mark Kostich; Page 4: © Roberto222, Manit321; Page 5: © pokosuke; Page 7: © Umut Cagri Tapici; Page 8: © olegmit1; Page 10: © Wikipedia; Page 11: © Steve Byland, Empire4191; Page 12: © Stephen McSweeny; Page 13: © John Cacalosi; Page 14: © Omar Ariff Kamarul Ariffin; Page 15: © Isabella Pfenninger; Page 16: © John Bell, Kim Taylor; Page 17: © Jost Gantar; Page 18: © Simon Hack; Page 19: © Todd Winner; Page 20: © Dan Cardiff, Antagain; Page 21: © czardases, luoman; Page 22: © Rikke68;

Edited by Precious McKenzie

Cover Design by Renee Brady
Interior Design by Tara Raymo

Library of Congress Cataloging-in-Publication Data

Greve, Tom
  Snakes / Tom Greve.
    p. cm. -- (Eye to Eye with Animals)
  ISBN 978-1-61741-776-4 (hard cover) (alk. paper)
  ISBN 978-1-61741-978-2 (soft cover)
  Library of Congress Control Number: 2011924821

Rourke Educational Media
Printed in the United States of America,
North Mankato, Minnesota

Scan for Related Titles
and Teacher Resources

Also Available as:

Rourke
Educational Media

rourkeeducationalmedia.com

customerservice@rourkeeducationalmedia.com • PO Box 643328 Vero Beach, Florida 32964

Table of Contents

Chapter 1
Monstrously Misunderstood

They are slithering, **scaly** and legless. Snakes are often portrayed as cold-blooded killers that give many people a serious case of the creeps. In reality, snakes pose little threat to humans.

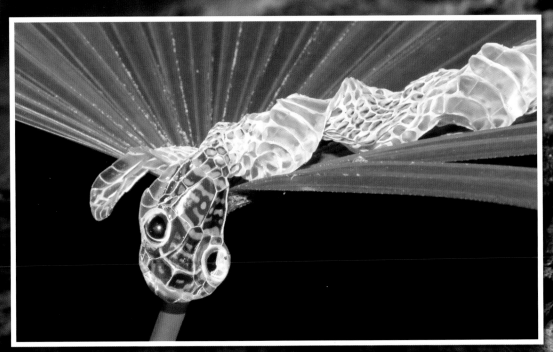

Like all animals, snakes' bodies grow as they get older, but their outer skin does not grow. As a result, snakes regularly shed their skin.

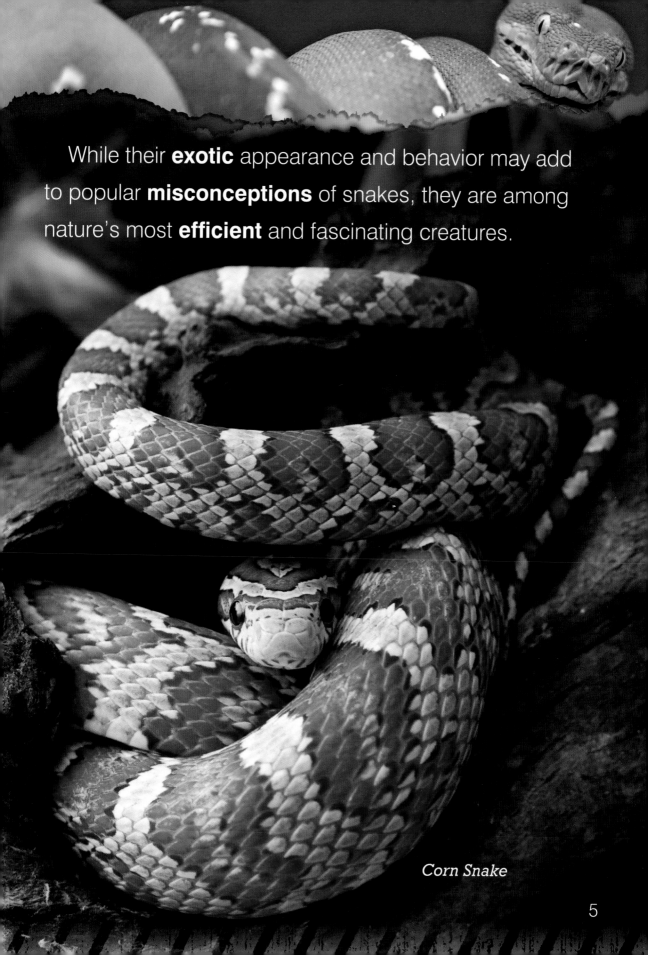

While their **exotic** appearance and behavior may add to popular **misconceptions** of snakes, they are among nature's most **efficient** and fascinating creatures.

Corn Snake

Chapter 2
Living Life Without Limbs

Snakes are a part of the reptile family of animals. All reptile **species** have scaly skin, a backbone, and are cold-blooded. But unlike most reptiles, snakes do not have arms or legs.

Where in the world do snakes live?

North America

Europe

Asia

Africa

South America

- Snake Range

Australia

Antarctica

There are about 3,000 different species of snakes on Earth. They live on every continent except Antarctica.

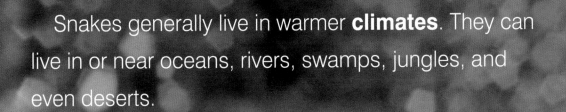

Snakes generally live in warmer **climates**. They can live in or near oceans, rivers, swamps, jungles, and even deserts.

◀◀

Snakes lie in the sun or coil their bodies to stay warm. They can use shade or water to stay cool. If it gets too cold, many snakes virtually shut down their body functions until warmer temperatures return.

Garter Snake

KNOWING HOW TO CHILL OUT

Cold-blooded animals like snakes are said to be ectothermic. This means that they cannot maintain their body temperature internally, they rely on their environment to keep their bodies warm or cool.

Snakes are among nature's best example of a species that has learned to pace itself. Like most reptiles, they use only as much energy as needed to stay warm, catch **prey**, and keep their own **predators** at bay.

Boa Constrictor

Part of snakes' amazing ability to conserve energy is their efficient digestive system. Once they've eaten, snakes can wait long periods of time before they get hungry again. This is especially true of larger snakes which typically eat large prey.

Snakes have **adapted** over millions of years into the limbless tubular **carnivores** we know them as today. They slither along the ground thanks to complex muscles attached to their **spine**.

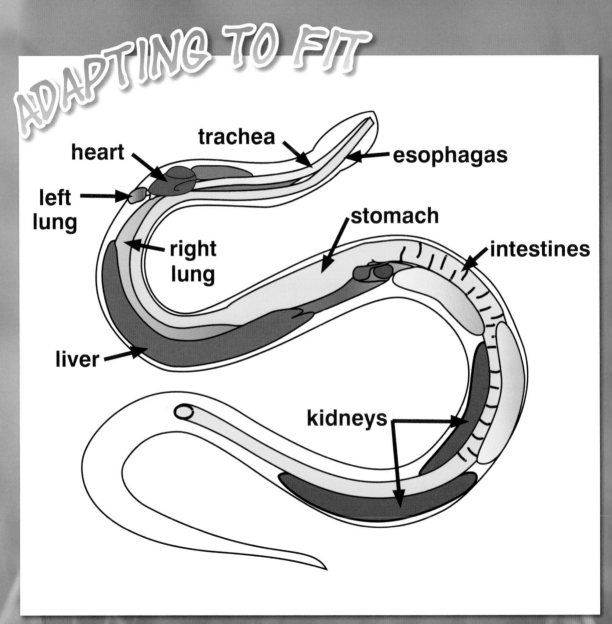

ADAPTING TO FIT

heart
trachea
esophagas
left lung
right lung
stomach
intestines
liver
kidneys

The internal organs of snakes are elongated and staggered rather than side-by-side so they can fit inside their long tube-shaped bodies.

Instead of relying on eyes and ears to see and hear, snakes rely on their forked tongues to sense danger or to find food.

Garter Snake

A snake's tongue is attached to its Jacobson's Organ – a sensory organ in the roof of its mouth which processes scents in the air caught by the tongue. Snakes do not have external ears and never close their eyes. Instead of moveable eyelids, they have special clear lenses to keep their eyes moist and protected.

CLAW ➡

Some snake species still have tiny, useless limbs that resemble a tiny claw. Scientists believe these are the leftovers of hind legs which they lost as they evolved from lizards.

11

Most snakes **reproduce** by laying eggs, especially those that live in warmer climates. But some snakes give birth to live young.

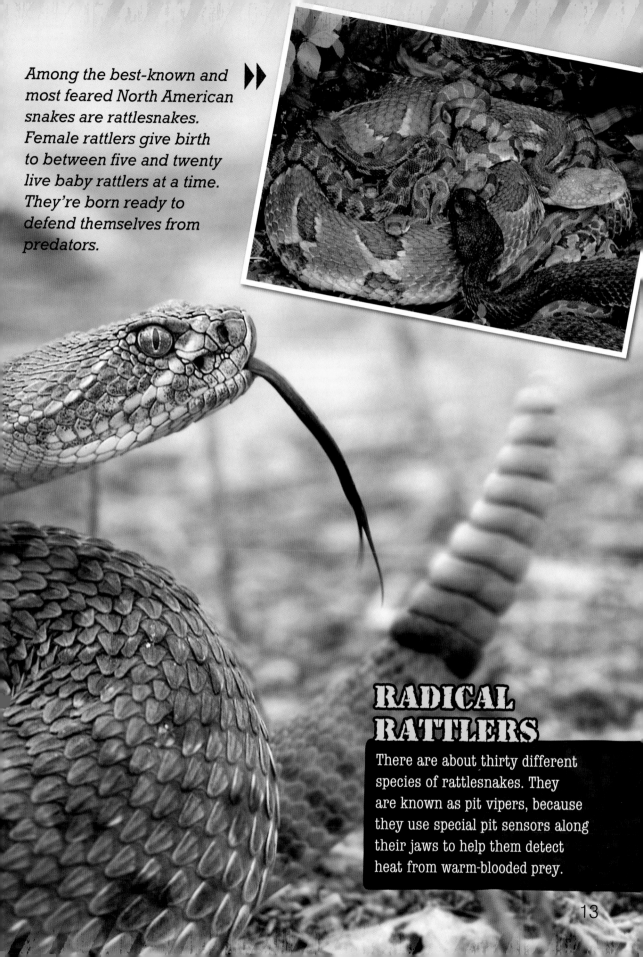

Among the best-known and most feared North American snakes are rattlesnakes. Female rattlers give birth to between five and twenty live baby rattlers at a time. They're born ready to defend themselves from predators.

RADICAL RATTLERS

There are about thirty different species of rattlesnakes. They are known as pit vipers, because they use special pit sensors along their jaws to help them detect heat from warm-blooded prey.

13

Chapter 3

Freaky Feasts

Despite having no arms or legs, snakes are incredibly shrewd and efficient hunters. All snakes are carnivores. Some snakes kill by biting and injecting toxic **venom** into their prey. Other snakes are constrictors. They attack by wrapping their long bodies around their prey and squeezing, or constricting, it to death.

The king cobra is the world's ▶▶ *longest venomous snake. Like rattlesnakes, king cobras inject venom into prey through their fangs. One toxic bite can kill much larger animals, but king cobras usually bite only as a defense when bothered. Don't worry, they only eat other snakes.*

Some snakes are passive hunters. They use their skin coloration to blend in with their surroundings as they wait for prey to come to them. Other snakes are active hunters. They move around looking for prey.

DESERT HORNED VIPER

A great example of passive hunting skill, the desert horned viper can hide its body under the sand of its desert habitat. Only its eyes remain above the sand, leaving it hidden from view of the small lizards it likes to eat.

In one of nature's most **bizarre** feeding routines, snakes swallow their prey whole. Many times, the prey is actually larger than the snake's head!

HOW DO THEY DO THAT?

Thanks to stretchable head muscles and the ability to unhinge their jaw bones, snakes can open their mouths wide enough to swallow animals that appear too big for them to eat. If humans did the same trick, we could easily swallow a basketball!

Amazon Tree Boa

Garter Snake

Not only can they unhinge their jaws, the skin on the underside of their lower jaw is highly stretchable.

KING-SIZED CONSTRICTOR

Green anacondas spend most of their lives in or near the swamps and rivers of northern South America. They can move easily through the water, but their massive weight makes them much slower on land.

Green anacondas are among the largest snakes on Earth and can grow to more than 30 feet (10 M) in length. They are constrictors and can swallow large mammals like deer and alligators, even humans if they feel threatened.

Chapter 4
Snakes in the Sea

Some species of snakes spend most of their lives in the salty water of the ocean. Like their cousins that live primarily on land, sea snakes have adapted to an underwater **habitat**.

Sea Snake

▲ *They live, hunt, and eat under water, but most sea snakes come out of the water to give birth. Baby sea snakes are born live.*

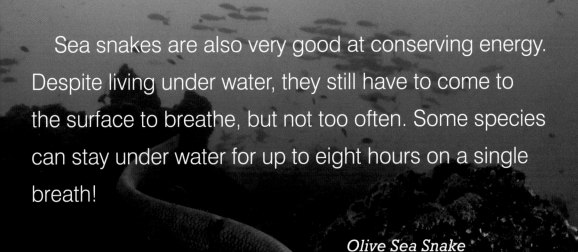

Sea snakes are also very good at conserving energy. Despite living under water, they still have to come to the surface to breathe, but not too often. Some species can stay under water for up to eight hours on a single breath!

Olive Sea Snake

SUPER SHEDDERS

Sea snakes shed their skin more frequently than other snakes. This helps get rid of algae or other ocean organisms that can attach themselves to a snake's skin.

Chapter 5

Threats and Conservation

The largest snakes have few, if any, predators. But most snakes have to avoid becoming a meal for other animals in their habitat. For many snakes, their greatest threat comes from the sky, rather than the ground.

SNAKESKIN SPECIAL

Some snakes are hunted by humans for their skins. They are also captured and sold as pets.

▲ *Large birds of prey like eagles and hawks swoop down and snatch up snakes for food.*

Human activities pose the greatest threat to snakes, but humans are also involved in helping th survive. **Conservation** groups like the Internationa Reptile Conservation Foundation work to ensure tha **endangered** species of snakes and other reptiles a protected along with their habitats.

BEWARE OF HUMAN

By far, the greatest threa to snakes is destruction of their habitat by humans. T is especially true in parts c the Amazon rainforest whe logging has reduced habitat space for many kinds of sna Many species are endangere

Little Tree Constrictor

Exotic, ectothermic, and efficient, snakes spend their lives eating, reproducing, and avoiding their predators while using only as much energy as needed.

Tough-skinned but vulnerable, bizarre but fascinating, snakes should be admired for their adaptability, not feared for their appearance.

Glossary

adapted (uh-DAPT-ed): able to change over time to accommodate a situation

bizarre (bi-SAR): strange, odd

carnivores (KAR-nuh-vorz): meat eaters

climates (KLYE-mits): the usual weather in certain places

conservation (kon-sur-VAY-shuhn): the protection of valuable or rare things

efficient (ee-FISH-uhnt): working well without wasting energy or resources

endangered (en-DAYN-jurd): in danger of disappearing or dying off as a species

exotic (eg-ZOT-ik): strange and fascinating

habitats (HAB-uh-tats): places and natural conditions where an animal lives

misconceptions (miss-kuhn-SEP-shunz): incorrect ideas about something

predators (PRED-uh-turz): animals that hunt other animals for food

prey (PRAY): an animal that is hunted by another animal for food

reproduce (ree-pruh-DOOSS): animals mating to make baby animals

scaly (SKAY-lee): covered in hard plates

species (SPEE-seez): groups into which animals are classified

spine (SPINE): backbone

venom (VEN-uhm): poison produced by some snakes, injected into prey by biting

Index

Websites To Visit

Nationalgeographic.org

Sandiegozoo.org

NationalZoo.si.edu

IRCF.org

seaworld.org

ReptileChannel.com

About the Author

Tom Greve lives in Chicago with his wife Meg and their children Madison and William. He loves the outdoors and loves to visit the snakes at Lincoln Park Zoo.

Meet The Author!
www.meetREMauthors.com